IMAGES OF WAR

HITLER'S

PROPAGANDA PILGRIMAGE

RARE PHOTOGRAPHS FROM WARTIME ARCHIVES

IMAGES OF WAR
HITLER'S
PROPAGANDA PILGRIMAGE

RARE PHOTOGRAPHS FROM WARTIME ARCHIVES

BOB CARRUTHERS

Pen & Sword
MILITARY

This edition published in 2015 by

Pen & Sword Military
An imprint of
Pen & Sword Books Ltd.
47 Church Street
Barnsley
South Yorkshire
S70 2AS

ISBN: 9781473833500

A CIP catalogue record for this book is available from the British Library.

Printed and bound in Malta
By Gutenberg Press Ltd

Pen & Sword Books Ltd. incorporates the imprints of Pen & Sword Aviation, Pen & Sword Family History, Pen & Sword Maritime, Pen & Sword Military, Pen & Sword Discovery, Pen & Sword Politics, Pen & Sword Atlas, Pen & Sword Archaeology, Wharncliffe Local History, Wharncliffe True Crime, Wharncliffe Transport, Pen & Sword Select, Pen & Sword Military Classics, Leo Cooper, The Praetorian Press, Claymore Press, Remember When, Seaforth Publishing and Frontline Publishing

For a complete list of Pen & Sword titles please contact

PEN & SWORD BOOKS LIMITED
47 Church Street, Barnsley, South Yorkshire, S70 2AS, England
E-mail: enquiries@pen-and-sword.co.uk
Website: www.pen-and-sword.co.uk

Contents

Chapter One

The Return to Flanders

The controversy surrounding Hitler's two visits to the Great War battlefields of northern France and Flanders has endured for over 70 years. The first visit took place on 1 June 1940, at the time of his visit the battle for France was continuing and the British were still fighting on the perimeter at Dunkirk only 40 miles away. Hitler, as supreme commander, made a routine visit to the Headquarters of von Richenau's 6th Army at Wevelgem, but the staff officers struggling with the logistics of the ongoing battle for Dunkirk must have been surprised to be required to suddenly make arrangements for the *Führer* to drive in a great loop through what was still a warzone. The sole purpose of the trip was to allow Hitler to visit some obscure towns and villages which no longer had strategic value in June 1940. The 1 June visit was unexpected and unnecessary, the circular trip was a frustrating diversion at a time when there were much more pressing calls on Hitler who, as supreme commander, was much in demand elsewhere especially with an undefeated French army still in the field.

The reason for Hitler's diversionary journey was obvious to any German soldier. The itinerary included Menen, Gheluvelt, Ypres, Langemark, Poperinge, Kemel and Wervick. These seemingly unimportant places were actually the sites of the battles of the Great War. This was where the ageing warriors of the *frontgemeinschaft* (the informal brotherhood of the trenches) had served from 1914-18. These towns and villages were the former locations of the front line trenches which had formed the Ypres salient.

Amazingly Hitler took with him Germany's most senior commanders. By 1 June 1940 it was apparent that the BEF was a beaten force and the withdrawal from Dunkirk was already underway. At a crucial time, with a strong French army still in the field, Generals Wilhelm Keitel and Alfred Jodl were required to join Hitler on what was little more than a glorified trip down memory lane. The RAF and the French Air Force were still operational and during his visit Hitler's party travelled in armoured Mercedes six-wheel staff cars which were guarded by SS men mounting MG 34 machine guns. They were also escorted by a mobile *Luftwaffe* air defence detachment mounting a 2cm flak cannon in case of air attack.

Although he cultivated the impression that he had been ever present in the trenches, Hitler knew the uncomfortable truth behind the myths surrounding his service in the Great War.

On the morning of 10 May 1940. Assault infantry gather before the attack.

Across the border. Tank obstacles could not stop the grenadiers of a Panzer Division.

Some bridges were blown but German assault engineers maintained the pace of the advance.

The infantry were at the forefront of the advance.

Anti-tank gunners on the look-out for enemy armour.

The artillery has done its duty. The infantry finishes the task. An assault troop is about to infiltrate.

Generalfeldmarschall Karl Rudolf Gerd von Rundstedt delivers a report to the *Führer*.

This is how the *Felsennest* ('Rocky Eyrie' headquarters) of the *Führer* was skilfully camouflaged.

Hitler with *Reichsmarschall* Göring and chief military adjutant, Colonel Schmundt, at a presentation.

The *Reichsmarschall* has appeared at headquarters to make a report.

Reichsmarschall Göring with the *Führer* at the 'Rocky Eyrie' headquarters.

Assault troops move up to the front.

Advance under burning heat. German fliers and German artillery have done a thorough job here.

Assault troops in a battle damaged town.

Hitler in a conference with his chief military adjutant, Colonel D. G. Schmundt.

The *Führer* and his Reich Press Chief, Dr. Dietrich.

Paratroopers and infantrymen of the airborne troops assemble for the attack on Rotterdam.

Paratroopers attack.

The Knights Cross direct from the hand of the *Führer*.

The *Führer* and the victors of Eban Emael.

Chapter Two

The 1 June Visit to Flanders

Despite his unspectacular rank, for Adolf Hitler, his service in the Great War was a matter of pride which occupied a place of towering significance in his life. By his own account in *Mein Kampf* it defined him as a man. It was in Flanders that Hitler had won the Iron Cross 2nd Class, an event which he described as the happiest day of his life. It was against this background that, despite all of the more pressing demands on his time, in June 1940, Hitler twice seized the opportunity to come back to Flanders and recapture the years he treasured. In the process he would, of course, make valuable political capital and shore up the myth that he was entitled to unconditional acceptance and pride of place in the informal ranks of the *frontgerneinschaft*.

On the first of those trips, on 1 June 1940, while the battle for France was still unfolding, Hitler and his entourage took a short flight to the *Luftwaffe* advance airfield at Evere. From here they mounted a fleet of six-wheeled Mercedes and drove in triumph through the deserted streets of Brussels. They then travelled on via Ghent to Ypres where they stopped in Kauwekijnstraat to view the Menin Gate.

The Menin Gate is the imposing monument to the 52,000 British war dead from this sector of the front who have no known grave. To this day the missing British soldiers are commemorated by a moving ceremony which takes place daily. When Hitler came to the town on 1 June 1940 the monument had been damaged by the recent fighting and there was, of course, no question of a ceremony in honour of the men of the British army. Hitler did pause respectfully to study the monument and was no doubt conscious of the fact that some of those men may well have been killed by the Bavarians of Hitler's own Regiment, but the visit to Ypres was brief as the real object of his visit was calling him northwards.

From Ypres Hitler and his entourage moved on to the German War Cemetery at Langemark which was the main stop on his tour. Today the cemetery is very much the same as it was in 1940, an oasis of sombre and dignified tranquillity. However on the day Hitler made his heavily escorted trip to view the graves of his fallen comrades the *Wehrmacht* had laid on a guard of honour and as word went round every off-duty soldier in the area swarmed to the site in the hope of grabbing a glimpse of the *Führer*. The presence of a film crew and Hoffmann's clicking cameras along with the jostling mob of sight-seeing *landsers* snapping away on their own cameras robbed the occasion of every shred of sombre dignity, but the publicity goals were achieved and the visit featured heavily in the June edition of *Deutsche Wochenschau*. In print the visit was prominently featured in the 13 June edition of the Nazi propaganda magazine *Illustreiter Beobachter*.

Escaping from the crush at Langemark Hitler and his entourage re-boarded their fleet of Mercedes armoured limousines and travelled south via Poperinge to Kemmel and ascended the local highpoint known as Kemmelberg (Kemmel Mountain). Here Hitler viewed the battlefields where his regiment had witnessed tough fighting on numerous occasions between 1914 and 1918 and map in hand was able to point out to his entourage the places where he had seen service.

Next day Hitler's entourage came south to Vimy near Arras where the List regiment had fought in 1916 and into 1917. For the genuine members of the *frontgemeinschaft* the collective memory was that the fighting in the German frontline during the battle was relentless and bloody. Their Canadian opponents suffered terribly and today those losses are commemorated by the preserved trenches and memorials.

However on 2 June 1940 it was the German *Führer* who strutted in triumph through Vimy Ridge. Hitler was accompanied throughout his tour by Willhelm Keitel, Germany's most senior Field Marshal. The irony can't have been lost on Keitel that he was now subordinate to a man who had only ever held the rank of *Gefreiter*.

Hitler's Surprise Visit to Flanders
1-2 June 1940

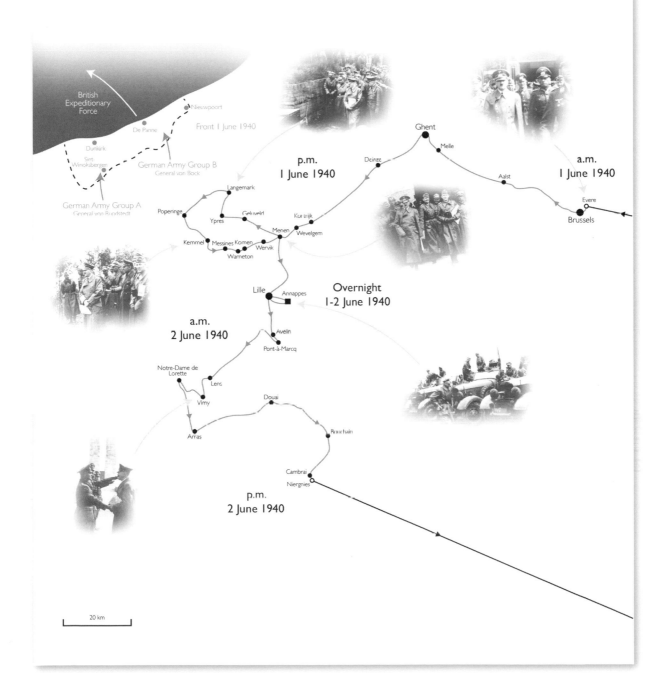

British
Expeditionary
Force

Nieuwpoort

Front 1 June 1940

De Panne

Dunkirk

Sint-
Winoksbergen

German Army Group B
General von Bock

German Army Group A
General von Rundstedt

Ghent

Melle

**p.m.
1 June 1940**

Deinze

Aalst

**a.m.
1 June 1940**

Langemark

Poperinge

Ypres

Geluveld

Kortrijk

Menen

Wevelgem

Evere

Brussels

Kemmel

Messines Komen

Wervik

Warneton

Lille

Annappes

**Overnight
1-2 June 1940**

**a.m.
2 June 1940**

Avelin

Pont-à-Marcq

Notre-Dame de
Lorette

Lens

Vimy

Douai

Arras

Bouchain

Cambrai

Niergnies

**p.m.
2 June 1940**

20 km

Hitler arrives at Evere airfield near Brussels. On the right of the *Führer* is the Commanding General of an Army Corps, General of the Infantry von Schwedler.

Generalfeldmarschall von Bock reports to Hitler, accompanied by *Generalfeldmarschall* von Brauchitsch.

The *Führer* is met by *Generalfeldmarschall* Kesselring. In the background, *Generalfeldmarschall* von Brauchitsch and *Generalfeldmarschall* von Bock.

In conversation with Senior General Strauss.

The *Führer* in conversation with *Generalfeldmarschall* von Kluge and Major-General Rommel, the Commander of the 7th Panzer division.

Meeting a Special Officer of a propaganda company. Behind them, *Generalfeldmarschall* von Reichenau and Lieutenant-General Bodenschatz.

On the morning of 1 June 1940 Hitler's entourage drive through Brussels passing the Tervurenlaan, the structure erected in the memory of King Leopold II in 1880.

During the flying visit the British Expeditionary Force was still fighting to maintain the Dunkirk perimeter. At the time this photograph was taken the nearest British unit was only 20 km distant.

The six-wheeled Mercedes type 770G-4 W31 was the vehicle favoured by Hitler, a fleet of these cars was placed at his disposal for the surprise visit to Flanders on 1 June 1940.

The Mercedes were guarded by SS men manning MG 34 machine guns. In this photograph, the column can be seen approaching the Brussels Palace of Justice.

A route was swiftly cleared through the bomb damaged towns of Flanders.

Senior General von Küchler of Army Group B makes a situation report to Hitler.

I   r thought following Küchler's report.

                                                    ime on 1 June in a wooded park near Melle some 10 km south

Hitler prided himself on taking simple meals in the field with his soldiers. He eschewed elaborate or ostentatious meals and felt that the officers should share the hardships of the men.

Still with Küchler and his staff, the military business now attended to, Hitler enjoys his customary light mid-day meal.

Speeding through Ghent at around 2 p.m. on 1 June 1940, Hitler is greeted in customary fashion by the hastily assembled German soldiery.

The medieval fortifications of Flanders are now in German hands. In this photograph, the Gravensteen castle is skirted by the fast moving entourage.

In the village of Deinze Hitler's entourage halted briefly to receive a situation report from Heinrich Himmler. Himmler is seen here hurrying towards Hitler's car as it draws to a halt.

Hitler's procession through Flanders is constantly recorded in stills by Hoffmann and on film by the men of the Propaganda Company (PK).

Hitler in ebullient mood arrives in Wevelgem for a conference with General von Reichenau.

It is now 3.00 p.m. and the entourage stops at the Headquarters of General von Reichenau.

The column presses on through Ypres watched by bemused townspeople.

A fleeting glimpse of Hitler seated in his favoured position of the front passenger seat.

Hitler and his entourage arriving in Kauwekijnstraat on the town side of the Menin Gate. This area has changed very little in the intervening years. To Hitler's right is his SS adjutant Heinz Linge, standing in the car is adjutant Julius Schwab. The driver is Erich Kempka.

Hitler parked in Kauwekijnstraat. The time is approximately 4 p.m. on 1 June 1940.

Another photograph of Hitler as he dismounts from his Mercedes in Kauwekijnstraat.

As the entourage look on Hitler takes the first step towards the Menin Gate.

A dark day for the allies, Hitler and Jodl outside the Menin Gate.

A reverse shot of Hitler leading his entourage into the chamber of the Menin Gate. The monument was erected to the British soldiers with no known grave who fell in defence of Ypres.

Hitler stands in silent contemplation of the vast monument to the British dead. The figure with his back to the camera is General Jodl.

Hitler leading the way as the entourage passes under the Menin Gate. The battle damaged scroll of honour to the British dead can be seen behind his right shoulder.

Hitler emerging from the Menin Gate, the battle damage suffered by town can be observed in the buildings behind him.

With the main sightseeing stop over the column heads on towards Langemark Cemetary.

Hitler arrived at Langemark Cemetery at around 4:30 p.m. By this time word had spread and the site was mobbed by off-duty German troops.

Hitler progresses past the respectful soldiery, to his right is General Viktor von Schwedler.

Hitler made his way towards the granite blocks which mark the last resting place of the young men who fell in the 1914 battle which is known to the Germans as the *kindermord*.

Hitler framed by the entrance to the cemetery.

This image first appeared in Hoffmann's book *'Mit Hitler Im Westen'*, and shows Hitler visiting the graves of German soldiers in Flanders. On Hitler's right is General of the Infantry von Schwedler.

Hitler pausing in silent remembrance as originally featured in *'Mit Hitler Im Westen'*.

Hitler standing behind the low wall of the cemetery gazes across, what was then, a sea of black crosses. The rotund figure on the right is Hoffmann.

The reverse view reveals the field of crosses which once characterised the Langemark cemetary.

Once more the car is mobbed by admirers.

The enthusiastic men of the *Wehrmacht* press forward for the chance to touch the hand of their esteemed leader.

The column then moved on to Mount Kemmel by way of Poperinge.

An abandoned British heavy gun is quickly forgotten as the cars speed towards the Kemmelberg.

An excellent study of the fleet of open Mercedes which ferried Hitler and his entourage around on 1 and 2 June 1940.

Hitler and Keitel on the summit of Mount Kemmel. Both men had served in the Great War, Hitler as a runner and Keitel as an artillery officer.

The swastika is raised over Mount Kemmel.

The Supreme Commander surveys the old battlefield of Mount Kemmel. During his four years of service Hitler was a frequent visitor to the Ypres battlefield. His wartime service began in October 1914 near Gheluvelt and ended near Ypres in October 1918 when he was gassed by a British shell.

Hitler observes the distant landmarks indicated to him by von Schwedler.

The cafe at the summit of Mount Kemmel still exists and can be visited today.

Hitler spent the night of 1-2 June in the Chateau at Annapes.

On the morning of 2 June the column set off once more, this time the main attraction was the former battlefield on Vimy Ridge.

The Commanding General of an Army Corps, General of the Artillery Heitz, explains to the *Führer* the course of the fighting of the last days, also present is the Army Commander, *Generalfeldmarschall* von Kluge.

Early on the morning of 2 June 1940 Hitler was joined by von Kluge for the tour of the Vimy Ridge memorial and battlefield. The only change that has since taken place is the addition of a handrail to the small concrete over-bridge.

Hitler's party inspect the magnificent Canadian monument on Vimy Ridge. The wooden structures behind were designed to protect the fragile statues from possible bomb damage.

Another image which appeared in *'Mit Hitler Im Westen'*. Here the entourage are seen passing the site of the old German front line.

Hitler points out some of the salient features of the battlefield. Hitler was very familiar with this terrain and was able to speak from personal experience.

Hitler leaving the Canadian monument at Vimy Ridge. He is flanked by Keitel and von Kluge.

Hitler congratulates Rommel on the achievements of his 7th Panzer Division.

Next on Hitler's agenda was a visit to the memorial on the nearby heights of Notre Dame de Lorette.

While Hitler and his entourage were parading round the former battlefields, the survivors of the recent battle for France were being marched into captivity.

Chapter Three

Hitler in the Great War

On the surface there was very little reason for the controversy which surrounds Hitler's service record in the Great War. The bald facts of Hitler's military career are very clear and reasonably well documented. At first glance it appears strange that there should be any debate whatsoever.

Hitler came to the Odeonsplatz on 2 August 1914 to celebrate the outbreak of the war against Russia. He stood near the front of the crowd who began to cheer and the moment was captured in this photograph by a Munich photographer called Heinrich Hoffmann. Hitler can be clearly seen in the Hoffmann photograph smiling and waving his hat.

France declared war on 3 August 1914 and the French declaration was followed, on 4 August 1914, by the British declaration of war. Overcome with war-fever Hitler enlisted as a volunteer and served in the 1st company of 16th Bavarian Reserve infantry regiment as a private soldier with the rank of *infanterist*.

Hitler and his regiment then moved by train to Belgium and first saw action in late October 1914 fighting against British troops from the Worcester Regiment in the grounds of the Chateaux near the village of Gheluvelt. The battle was a peripheral action during the battle known to the British as First Ypres, and to the Germans as Langemark. This violent action engagement was the only fight in which Hitler actually served with his rifle in hand as an *infanterist*. By the time of a short fight which followed near the village of Wytschaete, Hitler was already serving as a messenger and by 9 November 1914 was selected to serve in regimental headquarters in the position of regimental *meldegänger* (a military courier). There is no question however that, despite all that is written to the contrary, he did take part in at least that one battle.

In early November Hitler's regiment was again involved in an action, this time against the London Scottish who were supported by French troops. The fight took place at a location near the village of Wytschaete at the spot which was then known to the Bavarians as the 'axe-shaped' wood which is today known as the Bayernwald.

Following those two bloody engagements Hitler had distinguished himself as a reliable and trustworthy soldier and was rewarded by being promoted to the status of *Gefreiter*. He was also awarded the Iron Cross 2nd Class for saving the life of Lieutenant Colonel Englehardt in an incident near the Bayernwald. Much later, in 1932, Lieutenant Colonel Engelhardt reciprocated by taking Hitler's part in a successful court case brought by

Hitler in order to protect his reputation. The 1932 pamphlet entitled *Tatsachen und Lügen um Hitler* ('Facts and Lies About Adolf Hitler') which was published in the wake of the court case quotes Lieutenant Colonel Englehardt and describes Hitler's act of bravery which led to the award of the Iron Cross 2nd Class: "Once as I emerged from the wood at Wytschaete during a fierce attack, in order to make some observations, Hitler and an orderly from the Regimental Staff, planted themselves bang in front of me to shield me with their own bodies from machine-gun fire."

For the next two years Hitler served dutifully in Belgium and France. In 1915 he witnessed the vicious battles of Neuve Chapelle when the British took to the offensive. 1916 saw him in action at Aubers Ridge and on the Somme. In 1917 he was present at the battle of Arras and he was a witness to the fierce fighting for Vimy Ridge. In 1918 Hitler's regiment took part in the *Kaiserschlacht*, the last great German offensive of the war.

Hitler's role throughout the entire four years of the Great War involved him running messages between regimental Headquarters and the battalion headquarters both of which were set some way back from the front lines. As such he had an easier job than the company messengers who were actually stationed in the frontlines. Nonetheless during the course of his duties Hitler was on occasion required to carry messages into the trenches and he was frequently under fire. Even in the rear areas there was the ever present danger of a sudden long range shell. On the journey to and from battalion headquarters there were still plenty of bullets and shells for regimental messengers to contend with, and Hitler was considered lucky having avoided death and serious injury during two years of active service and in honour of his home town he was given the nickname 'Lucky Linzer' by his colleagues. A local legend is that Hitler was slightly wounded in 1916 and was treated in the crypt of the church at Messines. As a result he was inspired to paint the famous picture of the ruins of the church which, in later years, hung in his Munich office as a lucky talisman.

But in October 1916, on the Somme battlefield, near the town of Bapaume, his luck finally ran out and the 'Lucky Linzer' was seriously wounded by a shell splinter in the thigh. As a result he spent two months in hospital; following his recuperation Hitler once more returned to his own regiment and served at the front throughout 1917. The regiment fought on into 1918 and Hitler remained at his post and was awarded the Iron Cross First Class for conscientious and conspicuous devotion to duty including an extraordinary episode in which he is reported by witnesses to have captured a party of 15 French soldiers.

Finally in October 1918, in almost the last month of the war Hitler was temporarily blinded as a result of a British gas shell and ended the war in hospital in Paesewalk in Pomerania.

A Bavarian officer reading out the German declaration of war in August 1914.

On Sunday, 2 August 1914, a twenty-five year old Hitler was amongst thousands of people gathered at the Odeonsplatz in Munich. The crowd joined in exuberant enthusiasm for the war and Heinrich Hoffmann was on hand to record the scene. He later identified Hitler as a figure in the crowd.

Taken in April 1915 in Fournes, this is the earliest known photograph of *Regimentsordonnanzen* (Regimental Orderlies) including messengers Ernst Schmidt, Anton Bachmann and Adolf Hitler. Seated at Hitler's feet is the English Terrier, Foxl, who came to be Hitler's most treasured companion.

The conditions in the water-logged frontline trenches near Fromelles were appalling, as this photograph from May 1915 graphically demonstrates. The men of the 16th RIR lived and fought in these conditions.

(Below left) Max Amann (left) pictured at La Bassée station in March 1917. (Below Right) A German position at Fromelles, pre-1915. Trenches such as these were frequently knee-deep in water.

Adolf Hitler, then a battalion-messenger, seen in May 1915 with his rifle slung over his shoulder. Hitler was in the process of delivering a message. This photograph first appeared in the Official Regimental History of the 16th RIR.

(Below left) Adolf Hitler and Karl Lippert in mid-1915 in Fournes. (Below right) Adolf Hitler in 1916 in the rear area at Fournes.

Hitler with his comrades in September 1915, at the Regimental Command Post in Fromelles. (Front row, left to right) Adolf Hitler, Josef Wurm, Karl Lippert, Josef Kreidmayer. (Middle row, left to right) Karl Lanzhammer, Ernst Schmidt, Jacob Höfele, Jacob Weiss. (Back row) Karl Tiefenböck.

Early September 1916, Hitler is seen alongside his colleagues and his faithful dog Foxl in the rear area at Fournes. (Front row, left to right) Adolf Hitler, Balthasar Brandmayer, Anton Bachmann, Max Mund. (Back row, left to right) Ernst Schmidt, Johann Sperl, Jacob Weiss and Karl Tiefenböck.

Hitler with his comrades in May 1916 in Fournes: Balthasar Brandmayer (front), (left to right seated) Johann Wimmer, Josef Inkofer, Karl Lanzhammer, Adolf Hitler, (left to right standing) Johann Sperl, Max Mund.

The badly damaged town of Fromelles, where the Regimental Headquarters of the 16th RIR was situated from 17 March 1915 to 27 September 1916. Even in the rear areas, such as this, long-range shelling was a constant menace.

Chapter Four

The Controversy

With such an obvious and apparently flawless military record it is surprising that there should be any room for debate, but Hitler's record has come under attack for a wide variety of reasons. The case against Nazi portrayal of Hitler as a genuine and relentless frontline trench fighter was pursued by Hitler's opponents throughout the twenties and into the thirties. These rumours appeared freely in the German press and as long as the debate continued over Hitler's claim to be entitled to be counted as one of the frontline band of brothers who formed the *frontgemeinschaft*, the more the legend of Hitler the rear area malingerer took root and grew stronger.

Due to the overwhelming strength of the circumstantial evidence Hitler could not risk a fight with those papers which habitually referred to him as an Austrian draft dodger. Finally however, in 1932, the SDP supporting newspaper *Echo Der Woche* stepped over the mark by mistakenly labelling him a 'deserter' from the Austrian army. Hitler knew this was untrue and in order to protect his precarious reputation he was able to take court action, safe in the knowledge that he could not loose. His court victory was the catalyst for the 1932 pamphlet entitled *Tatsachen und Lügen um Hitler* which reprinted the testimony of many of his former colleagues concerning the war service of Adolf Hitler.

The controversy was to an extent self-inflicted, and began in Munich in 1913 with Hitler's initial failure to attend for service in the Austro-Hungarian army. Almost a century later the debate still continues, was Hitler a brave and dedicated warrior as his war record suggests? Or was he in fact a coward and a malingerer who had run away from his native Austria to avoid conscription and who ended up hiding from danger in the rear areas?

Hitler himself played a major role in causing the events which perpetuated a century debate. In 1913 he moved abruptly to Munich from his native Austria. This sudden flight was highly suspicious as his precipitate move took place shortly after he was due for service in the Austro-Hungarian army. As a result of Hitler's rapid departure the circumstantial evidence was insurmountable and the popular conception was easily fostered that Adolf Hitler was a coward who ran away from Austria to Germany in 1913 in order to avoid military service.

The suspicion that Hitler had something to hide was compounded by the fact that in the pages of *Mein Kampf* he deliberately gave a false date for his move to Munich. Hitler claimed that he moved to Munich in 1912. Had it been true, this statement would have provided him with some cover against the charge that his move to Germany was simply an attempt to avoid military service as he could claim that he had already moved to Germany long before his Austrian call up in 1913. Fortunately for Hitler he was deemed to be medically unfit and thereby legitimately escaped conscription into the Austro-Hungarian army. In 1932 in order to silence his detractors Hitler actually obtained an official statement from the Austrian government.

Office of the State Government, State Registry Office, Nr. 786
Official Statement
 Adolf Hitler, born on 20 April 1889 in Braunau am Inn and resident of Linz, Upper Austria, son of Alois and Klara (maiden name, Plötzl), was found by examination of the 3rd age group in Salzburg on 5 February 1914 to be "too weak for military or support service," and was declared "unfit for military service".

Linz, 23 February 1932,
signed Opitz

Following his narrow brush with conscription Hitler spent a happy year working as an artist in Munich, but by 1914 war clouds were gathering over Europe and it is here that the Hitler story takes another remarkable twist.

Although he was an Austrian and technically barred from serving in the German armed forces Hitler volunteered for service in the Bavarian army. In the chaos surrounding the outbreak of war he was somehow accepted and was enlisted in the ranks of the newly raised reserve infantry regiment 'List' named after its commander Major Julius List.

There is no question that the account of the battle around Gheluvelt in *Mein Kampf* is substantially true. However, the awkward truth for the Nazi spin doctors was the fact that this was the only battle he took part in as a fighter.

There is no question that the men on the regimental staff had a comparatively easy life to what was endured by the men in the trenches. The 16th Bavarian RIR had an establishment of 3000, but over 3700 men were killed serving in its ranks, the vast majority from the front line trenches companies. On the other hand, although there were substantial casualties among the runners in 1914, Hitler and most of his tight-knit group of comrades who served in the regimental HQ of the 16th RIR, and who were pictured together in 1916, actually survived the war.

With such a high level of casualties in the frontline companies, there were ample opportunities for promotion, but Hitler was never promoted beyond the rank of *Gefrieter*, which loosely approximates to a lance corporal. According to Sergeant Max Amann who was interrogated after the war, Hitler was offered the prospect of promotion to the rank of *Korporal* but begged to be allowed to remain in the role of regimental *meldegänger*. It is now widely accepted that Hilter's motivation was self-interest and self-preservation and these were the factors that governed his decisions. Increased pay and *Korporal* status brought with them the risk of increased danger and discomfort. Hitler knew he had a relatively cushy job and he was determined to hold on to that job.

By 1917 Hitler had recovered from his wounds, however on returning to the front it was obvious that the Imperial German army was under intolerable strain. Constant shell-fire, malnutrition, disease, fatigue, nervous strain, sniper bullets, trench mortars, machine gun fire, plagues of rats, mines and lice were the ever present companions in the trenches. By and large Hitler was able to avoid the worst of these horrors. Comfortably billeted behind the lines in Fournes and elsewhere, Hitler didn't have to face the nightly terror of the possibility of an enemy trench raid or the chilling prospect of being sent on a trench raid of his own. Most nights he could sleep in a bed, draw hot rations and enjoy the comradeship of his close knit group of colleagues.

The plain fact was that, with the exception of the opening battle of his regiment's war at Gheluvelt, Hitler had served for the duration of the Great War as a *meldegänger* in the Headquarters of the 16th Bavarian Reserve Infantry Regiment, known to its members as the List Regiment in honour of its first commander, Major Julius von List. From all of the evidence available to us it would appear that the fighting for the farm at Becelare and Gheluvelt in late October and early November 1914 was the only occasion on which Hitler fought with rifle in hand. By the time of brief action against the London Scottish near Wytschaete in early November he was already serving as a regimental messenger. However the brief combat at Gheluvelt was enough for Hitler to distinguish himself in the field. It is possible that even during his first taste of fighting near Gheluvelt Hitler was already entrusted to carry messages in the field. If that was the case it is not beyond the bounds of possibility that he may never have fired a shot in anger. He had not in fact ever been a trench fighter, and in truth had never served a single day in a frontline trench. However, Hitler was first and foremost a politician; he was not one to miss a photo opportunity which was worth its weight in gold in propaganda terms. The film and photographic record of his trip would help him to convey the impression that he had constantly been in the thick of things.

In any event, his service record was sound. He carried out the duties assigned to him to the satisfaction of his commander. In recognition for his service as a runner, by 9 November 1914 he was selected to serve permanently at Regimental headquarters. He recorded the details of his new position in a letter to Ernst Hepp the Munich lawyer who had helped him when he had fallen foul of the military authorities in Vienna over his call up to the ranks of the Austro-Hungarian army. 'My job now is to carry dispatches for the staff. As for the mud, things are a bit better here, but also more dangerous. In Wytschaete during the first day of the attack three of us eight dispatch riders were killed, and one was badly wounded. The four survivors and the man who was wounded were cited for their distinguished conduct. While they were deciding which of us should be awarded the Iron Cross, four company commanders came to the dugout. That meant that the four of us had to step out. We were standing some distance away about five minutes later when a shell slammed into the dugout, wounding Lieutenant Colonel Engelhardt and killing or wounding the rest of his staff. This was the most terrible moment of my life. We worshiped Lieutenant Colonel Engelhardt.'

The fact that Hitler had distinguished himself in the early fighting was also recognised by him being awarded *Gefreiter* status. In the English speaking world the term *Gefreiter* as it applied to the Bavarian army of 1914 is problematic and has caused some difficulties in interpreting the Hitler story.

Over the centuries the German military tradition has harnessed a variety of incentives to encourage good conduct in the ranks. One of these was to recognise reliable private soldiers (who were known by the title *infanterist* in the Bavarian army) and rewarding them with an easier life. The word *Gefreiter* evolved from older German and Dutch – meaning "freed' or 'liberated' person. The title *Gefreiter* brought with it a series of a negative rights which meant the *Gefreitene* did not to have to perform many of the most menial duties which the private soldiers loathed so much. The holder of the title *Gefreiter* was freed from sentry duty. It is important to realise that *Gefreiter* was not a rank as such but merely a signifier of the status of a trustworthy private soldier, the revised status also brought with it a tiny rise in pay. An *infanterist* received 70 pfennigs per day while a *Gefreiter* received 75 pfennigs.

In the Bavarian army of 1914 the rank of corporal was the directly equivalent rank of *Korporal*. In the Prussian army the equivalent term was *Unteroffizier*. It is clearly a substantial error to translate *Gefreiter* to Corporal, but that is what so often happens. It is important to note that, in the Bavarian army of 1914, *Korporal* was the lowest rank from which orders could be given to subordinates. The *"Gefreitene"* on the other hand, although they were recognised as reliable private soldiers, had no power of command other men. The holder of the title remained an ordinary private soldier nonetheless and was not authorised to give any form of command.

Hitler's contemporaries such as Ignatz Westenkirchner, Hans Mend and Balthasar Brandmayer understood the sub-text of the situation and in the inter-war translations of Nazi books such as Heinz's 'Germany's Hitler', Hitler is consistently referred to as a private and on one occasion as a lance corporal. Alexander Moritz Frey however unfailingly refers to Hitler as a 'Private' and indeed this appears in the title of the unpublished article The Unknown Private Personal Memories of Hitler which came to light after the war.

In order to get round this difficulty the term *Gefreiter* is frequently equated with the British rank of lance corporal, but it is not altogether helpful as there was no direct equivalent in the Bavarian army. The mistaken assumption that a 1914 Bavarian *Gefreiter* was equivalent to an non-commissioned officer took root during World War II. By 1940 the role of the *Gefreiter* in the *Wehrmacht* had changed to a role which was indeed equivalent to a junior non-commissioned officer such as a lance corporal. The upshot of this difficulty in translation has led to the creation of the popular myth that Hitler was promoted with the equivalent rank of *unteroffizier* or *korporal*, this is simply untrue. Of one thing we can be certain Hitler never was a corporal.

Hitler (left with helmet), and next to him Balthasar Brandmayer, pose for the camera in a bunker near the frontline section of Reincourt-Villers in September 1916.

Hitler on 26 October 1916, in the Prussian Association of the Red Cross hospital in Beelitz near Berlin, where he was brought after being wounded on 5 October 1916.

Members of the POW camp guard contingent at Traunstein taken in early January 1919. Hitler (left circle) and Ernst Schmidt (right circle) served here guarding Russian POWs until 11 February 1919.

From 20 February to 8 March 1919, Hitler (seen standing in the centre at the rear of the photograph) helped to guard the Munich Central Train Station, he is pictured here with his fellow guards.

From soldier to *Führer*. These portraits illustrate the change in Hitler's face and moustache between the years of 1915 to 1921. (Left to right) Hitler pictured in 1915, 1916, 1919 and 1921.

The remains of the German trenches at Wytschaete near Ypres. Hitler served on this sector of the front and was awarded the Iron Cross 2nd Class for his actions at almost this exact spot.

The remains of a German block house at the Bayernwald near Ypres. Hitler spent the war carrying messages to and from locations such as this.

Chapter Five

Facts and Lies About Hitler

What we can be reasonably certain off is the fact that Hitler was a brave and conscientious soldier. In 1932 extracts from the testimonies provided by Hitler's colleagues in support of his libel action against *Echo Der Woche* were collected and published in the *Facts and Lies About Hitler* pamphlet and they appear to be absolutely genuine and truthful. They certainly stood up to scrutiny and were obviously strong enough to convince the court of Hitler's case. These sworn statements were each verified on oath and survived the rigours of the German legal system at a time before Hitler had tasted power. There is no question therefore of any legal fix and we must therefore accept the verdict of the court. It is clear from the weight of support that Hitler was certainly not, as he is all too frequently depicted, the cowardly and lonely outcast devoid of friends and lacking in respect from his comrades. In the pamphlet the statements are printed in order of rank with the most senior appearing first, beginning with the testimony of Colonel Satny.

'… I can only give former Corporal Hitler the greatest praise for his extraordinary accomplishments. Fournes was a village behind the regiment's battle line. It served as a recovery area for battalion relieved from the front, and also served as the seat of the regimental staff during calmer periods. The village was within the danger zone, and was frequently under rather heavy fire. During battle, the regimental headquarters was moved about 3/4 of an hour forward to Fournelles, and orders had to be carried to the front line. The path was often under enemy machine gun and artillery fire. I can never remember a single time when Hitler was absent from his post. Hitler may wear the medals he earned with pride…'

Signed: Satny, Colonel (retired),
former commander of the Bavarian R.-F.-R. 16 (List).

'Mr. Hitler, as corporal, was a courier for the regimental staff, and was not only always willing to carry out hard tasks, but did so with distinction. I stress that the List Regiment, as might be expected from its history, was at the toughest parts of the front, fighting in frequent major battles…'

Signed: Baligand, Colonel (retired),
last commander of the Bavarian R.-F.-R. 16 (List).

'… At particularly dangerous points I often was asked for volunteers, and at such times Hitler regularly volunteered, and without hesitation…'

Signed: Bruno Horn,
Lieutenant with the Bavarian R.-F.-R. 16 (List).

'… Hitler never hesitated in the least in carrying out even the most difficult order, and very often took on the most dangerous duties for his comrades.

Couriers for the regimental staff had to be among the most reliable people, because serving as a regimental courier during battles and skirmishes required iron nerves and a cool head. Hitler always did his duty, and even after his severe thigh wound, volunteered to be sent back to his regiment from the reserve battalion immediately after his release from the hospital…'

Signed: Max Amann,
former sergeant with the Bavarian R.-F.-R. 16 (List).

'… I often met Corporal Adolf Hitler as he served as courier to and from the front. Anyone who understands the duties of a courier – and any soldier who has served at the front does – knows what it means, day after day and night after night to move through artillery fire and machine gun fire from the rear…'

Signed: Joseph Lohr,
officer candidate with the Bavarian R.-F.-R. 16 (List).

'… It is true that Hitler was nearly blinded by a courier mission during a heavy gas attack, even though he was wearing a gas mask…'

Signed: Jakob Weiß,
NCO with the Bavarian R.-F.-R. 16 (List).

'… Hitler received the Iron Cross, First Class, during the spring or summer of 1918 for his outstanding service as a courier during the great offensive of 1918, and in particular for his personal capture of a French officer and about 15 men, whom he suddenly encountered during a mission, and as a result of his quick thinking and decisive action, captured.

Hitler was seen by his fellow couriers, and many others in the regiment, as one of the best and bravest soldiers.'

Signed: Ernst Schmidt,
with the Bavarian R.-F.-R. 16 (List) from November 1914 until October 1918.

According to the pamphlet, the most sensational moment of the trial came during the testimony of Hitler's regimental comrade Michael Schlehuber. Schlehuber was a Social Democrat and had been a trade union member for 35 years. He was certainly not a Nazi and was actually called as a witness by the opposing side; it was to prove a disastrous decision for Hitler's opponents:

'I have known Hitler since the departure for the front of the Bavarian R.-I-R. 16. I came to know Hitler as a good soldier and faultless comrade. I never saw Hitler attempt to avoid any duty or danger. I was part of the division from first to last, and never heard anything then or afterwards bad about Hitler. I was astonished when I later read unfavorable things about Hitler's service as a soldier in the newspapers. I disagree entirely with Hitler on political matters, and give this testimony only because I highly respect Hitler as a war comrade.'

Signed: Michael Schlehuber

The *Führer* initially directed the German military operations from this site deep in the Ardennes.

The second *Führer* headquarters 'Wolf's Lair'.

Reichsmarschall Göring leaves the 'Wolf's Lair' headquarters after reporting to the *Führer*.

At headquarters, the *Führer* briefs his old comrade Minister Rudolf Hess on the situation.

Reichsmarschall Göring takes his leave from Hitler in order to return in the 'Stork' to his headquarters.

In the 'Wolf's Lair'. The Supreme Commander of the Army reports new successes to the *Führer*.

Generalfeldmarschall von Brauchitsch at a conference. From left to right: Major Deyhle, General of the Artillery Jodl, the Supreme Commander of the Army von Brauchitsch, Grand Admiral Dr. H. C. Raeder. Far left: *Generalfeldmarschall* Keitel.

In the 'Wolf's Lair', Emissary Hewel of the Foreign Office gives the *Führer* a report.

On the path to the map room. Grand Admiral Dr. H. C. Raeder and *Generalfeldmarschall* Brauchitsch have come for a conference.

The *Führer* in the 'Wolf's Lair'.

New reports have come. The *Führer* plots them on the map himself.

After the morning situation report in the 'Wolf's Lair'. In the background the house of the Armed Forces Leadership Staff.

After the peace offer of the French.

Compiègne, 1940.

The *Führer* at the memorial stone that was designed to immortalise the humiliation of 1918.

The French delegation poses in front of the historic railcar for the beginning of the negotiations.

On 21 June, the *Führer* receives the French delegation.

Generalfeldmarschall Keitel reads aloud the *Führer's* preamble.

To the sound of the German National Anthem, the *Führer* leaves the site of the negotiations.

Hitler and his entourage hear the announcement of the pending truce over the radio.

'Germany, Germany above all!'

Proclamation of the truce in the *Führer's* headquarters on 25 June, 1940, 01:35.

Chapter Six

Hitler in Paris

On Sunday 23 June 1940 Adolf Hitler returned to France for his infamous visit to Paris. He was accompanied by his favoured architects Albert Speer and Hermann Giesler. The artistic aspect of the party was completed by the addition of Arno Breker, Hitler's most favoured sculptor. Both Giesler writing in 'Ein Anderer Hitler' and Breker in his memoirs state that the trip took place on Sunday 23 June. However, writing in his book 'Inside the Third Reich' Speer erroneously cites the date as 28 June 1940, but as he describes the moment when the armistice came into effect as part of the trip the date of 28 June is clearly an error on his part. Giesler later recalled how surprised he was to be stopped by the Viennese police and escorted to Vienna airport where he was placed on a courier aircraft bound for France. However there was a purpose behind Hitler's decision to include the artists. At a personal level Hitler cared nothing for the legendary city and was only interested in Paris for its architecture. The civilian members of his entourage were there to envision how the city could be outdone by the new Berlin visualised by Hitler as the greatest and most imposing city in the world. In order to blend into the background the artist and architects were equipped with military uniforms.

Accompanied by this unusual entourage and a film crew Hitler toured the deserted streets of the French capital in the early hours of that infamous Sunday morning.

We are fortunate to have a complete record of the day which was published in the book 'Ein Anderer Hitler' by Hermann Giesler which contains a full eye-witness description of his famous visit to Paris on 23 June, 1940. In the process Giesler also provides a full account of his own personal conversations with Hitler concerning sweeping architectural plans for the cities of Berlin, Munich and Linz which it was envisaged would embody the concept Grossdeutschland (Greater Germany).

Giesler begins when he was stopped by a police detail on 22 June, 1940 when on his way to a building site near Vienna, and ordered to drive to the Vienna airport. There, he boarded a waiting Ju. 52 courier airplane which landed on an airstrip in northern France, after which he was driven to Adolf Hitler's headquarters at Brûly-de-Peche, north of Sedan. The armistice was set to begin the following day at midnight. As soon as they met Hitler lost no time in relating his personal views to Giesler concerning his great triumph and his desire to see Paris as soon as possible.

'All right, Giesler, at that time you had no way of knowing, but I was confident of my strategic plan, the essential tactical details, and my belief in the fighting power of the German armed forces. From there, the wisely planned timetable advanced naturally. I recall that during the winter [of 1939] I invited you to go with me to Paris; I've invited Breker and Speer to come along. With my artists, I want to look at Paris. We will set off early in the morning.'

In company with Arno Breker and Albert Speer, Hitler, along with his staff and aides-de-camp, enjoyed a simple dinner together at two long tables in a simple cottage. Giesler was struck by the lack of triumphalism.

'There was no triumphant attitude, no booming voices – only sombre dignity. The faces of those in authority still bore the signs of the strain of the past weeks. I considered myself undeserving of the honour of sitting with them.'

The party set off from Brûly-de-Peche at 4 a.m. in the *Führer's* private Ju. 52 and landed at Le Bourget airport, where a fleet of open-topped Mercedes awaited them. Hitler took his usual place in the front passenger seat and was joined by Speer, Breker, Giesler, SS Adjutant Schaub and his ordinance officer, Colonel Speidel.

'The former military attache in Paris drove ahead of us as guide. With our dimmed lights we could only see the silhouettes of the buildings. We passed check points – the guards stepped out and saluted; one could detect that the armistice was not yet fully in force. Adolf Hitler sat in front of me and I remembered the past winter evening when he talked about Paris, and I recalled his confidence that he would view the city soon. Now his wish was coming true. But he did not come to Paris as the Supreme Commander of the German *Wehrmacht* – he arrived as the *Bauherr* (construction chief) of the new German cities which he already envisioned with their new aspects. He came here to compare architecture, to experience the atmosphere of the city in the company of his two architects and one sculptor, even though we were accompanied by a military entourage – soldiers who had certainly gained the honour of seeing the French capital with him.'

The stop on the brief tour of Paris was the Imperial Opera House. This magnificent structure was designed by the architect Garnier. Adolf Hitler had familiarised himself with the plans of the building and seemed keen to show off his knowledge. Inside the building, Giesler recalled that it was Hitler who led the way, pointing out noteworthy features of the building.

'It might be that the disparity between the simple atmosphere of the *Führer* headquarters in the tiny village of Bruly to this splendid display of the historic Empire amplified the impression it made. Till that point, I was only familiar with the Opera façade and was astonished by the well thought out notion of the basic plan, impressed by the lay out of the expansive rooms: the entry halls, the lavish staircase, the foyers and the splendid, lustrous, gold inner theatre. We were standing in the middle loge. Adolf Hitler was captivated – delightful, remarkably attractive proportions, and what festivity! It was a theatre with a distinct charisma, regardless of its extravagance of the "Belle Epoque" and a stylish diversity including a hint of over-the-top baroque. Hitler repeated that its main reputation rests on these beautiful proportions. "I would like to see the reception room, the salon of the President behind the proscenium box," said Hitler. A certain amount of hesitation took place. "According to Garnier's plan, it must be about here." The guard was at first muddled, but then he recollected that following a renovation the room was removed. Hitler acidly observed, "The democratic republic doesn't even favour its President with his own reception salon."

Hitler and his entourage then came out the front entrance in order to view the famous façade in daylight. They then moved on to the Madeleine, which did not move Hitler and the entourage was soon on the move through the deserted streets. 'Slowly, in a wide circle, we drove around the fountains and the Luxor obelisks at the Place de la Concord. Adolf Hitler stood up in his car to obtain a panoramic view. He gazed across the large square toward the Tuileries and the Louvre, then across the Seine River to the building of the Chambre des Députés. At the beginning of the Champs-Élysées, he asked to stop. Gazing at the walls of the Admiralty, he could now observe the column gable of the Madeleine through the short street space of the Rue Royal, it was now really effective.

Adolf Hitler took his time to absorb all this – then a brief signal with his hand and we drove slowly along the somewhat rising Champs-Élysées towards the Étoile with its commanding Arc de Triomphe. Critically appraising everything, his eyes looked at the road construction, which he could see through the tree-lined streets around the Round Point. All his absorbed concentration was on the Arc and the road system on which the surrounding area of the Étoile was planned. He took in the reliefs on the right and left side of the Arc with one short glance (they capture the story of the Marseillaise), and the chiselled inscriptions (the French would not forget any of their victorious battles). He knew every detail from historical literature.

Adolf Hitler shared his thoughts about this early morning journey with Geisler who later recorded what Hitler had said to him.

'The well-appointed expanse of the Place de la Concord impresses naturally since the square extends to the Tuileries Gardens to the Louvre, with views over the lower course of the Seine all the way to the ministries and the Chambre des Députés. Optically, it also includes the development towards the Madeleine and the wide open space of the start of the Champs-Élysées. From a man's perspective, that's nearly limitless. The view from the Concorde was beautiful, with its fountains and obelisk in the foreground, toward the Admiralty, the rue Royal with the Madelein in the background.'

From the Étoile they drove to the Trocadero, viewing the colossus of the 19th Century, the Eiffel Tower, across the Seine from the large terrace of the Palais Chaillot. It was here that Hoffmann took his iconic photographs which feature Geisler and Hitler. Giesler recalled that he entered into a long conversation with Hitler at that point in the proceedings.

'Adolf Hitler told me that he considers the Eiffel Tower not only as the beginning of a new standard of buildings, but also as the start of an engineering type of tectonics.

"This tower is not only synonymous with Paris and the world exhibition at that time, but it will stand as an example of classicism, and marks the commencement of a new era." By this he meant the era of modern technology with new horizons and dimensions (*Groessenordnungen*), at that time unachievable. What came next were wide-spanned bridges, buildings with large vertical dimensions which because of exact engineering calculations could now form iconic structures. But only through harmonisation between engineers, artists and architects could he see the possibility of enhanced creativity. Classicism, which we have to aim at, can only be reached by tectonics with new materials – steel and reinforced concrete indeed being definitive and essential.

'We drove on and stopped briefly at a well-proportioned city palais, which was to be the future German embassy. Adolf Hitler gave particular orders for its renovation with the support of French conservators.

'Adolf Hitler next showed his disappointment with the Pantheon at the top of the Latin Quarter by leaving the building abruptly. Out in the open again, he shook his head and heaved a sigh.

"'My God, it does not deserve its name, if you think about the Roman Pantheon with its classical interior, the unique lighting from the wide open ceiling – it combines dignity with gravity. And then you look at that" – and he pointed back – "more than sombre even on this bright summer day." As they returned to their car, a few women spotted them, crying out: c'est lui – that's him.

'We turned around and drove through the rue de Castiglioni to the Place Vendôme, with its famous column on this magnificently shaped square, then the rue de la Paix to the Place de l'Opéra, with a lofty view of the vivid, although somewhat theatrical, facade of the Opera, now in bright light. "Certainly," he said to me later; "it is very decorative, a bit too rich, but obviously conforming to the style taste of that era. In planning our architecture, we will aim at a classicism of sterner, sharper forms, according to our character. What I have seen in Paris forces me to compare the achievements of the German architecture of the same period: Gilly, Schinkel, Klenze, Hansen and Semper, and Siccardsburg with his Vienna Opera – I am of the opinion that they can hold their place. Not to mention the great creations of the baroque architects like Lukas Hildebrandt, Fischer von Erlach, Balthasar Neumann, Prandtauer and others. What the Germans miss is continuity and persistence in their architectural aims, but this is still recognizable in the Germany of the Middle Ages with cathedrals and domes of the city communities, and the baroque buildings of the royal houses.'"

Geisler next recalled the trip to Montmartre where Hitler barely glanced at the Sacré Cœur. From the elevated terrace in front of the church, he wanted to consider the vista of Paris he had just visited. 'Adolf Hitler believed that, as far as he could view the concentration of Paris from here, the monuments and places stood out only weakly from the monotony of living quarters and functional buildings. The great cohesion from the Louvre to the Étoile, the Île-de-France with the Notre Dame, the flowing of the Seine to the Eiffel tower is just barely maintained. Actually, only this tower, meant and built for an exhibition, maintains – regardless of its filigree transparency seen from here – its reputation. What he said is that the Tower justifies its existence in this city only by the deliberately planned vertical tendency – an astonishing feature for that epoch. Naturally, for the city of Paris it meant a symbolic novelty, a city with such a deep historical tradition from the Romans to the very significant eras of the kings, the revolution, the empire, the buildings of the republic after Napoleon III; they are all meaningless, of no importance for the overall structure of the city – with the exception of the Eiffel Tower.'

Entry of German troops into Paris on 15 June, 1940. German artillery on the Place de la Concorde.

A Regimental Commander receives the march past.

Men from Lower Saxony at the Arc de Triomphe.

A stroll through the Paris opera house.

Hitler pictured alongside Speer, Breker and Giesler. The Eiffel Tower can be seen in the background.

Hitler photographed on the Trocadero. In the background the Eiffel Tower.

Chapter Seven

Hitler and Napoleon

'We then stopped at a monument to a French general of the 1914-18 war with an inscription abusing German soldiers – very distasteful. Hitler got annoyed, waited for the accompanying car to stop, turned to the military men and ordered they see to it that it was blown up. In honour of Colonel General Keitel, who was travelling with us, we visited the Cour d'honneur de l'École militaire. Then we arrived at the highpoint of our trip – at least for me.

'In the dome of Les Invalides, Adolf Hitler stood at the edge of the rim of the crypt for a long time. His head was bent as he stared down at Napoleon's sarcophagus. I stood at his left side, not by accident, but because he dragged me to his side. Quietly he said to me, "Giesler, you will build my grave site, we'll talk about it later."

'Quiet and in reflective mood, he left the dome; we remained a few steps behind him. Outside the gate, Hitler turned around: "Bormann, I want the Herzog of Reichsstadt to be brought back to Paris." The Herzog was Napoleon's son from his marriage second wife, the Austrian Princess Marie Luise. He was brought up in Vienna and educated there. He died in 1832 at the age of twenty-one at the Schoenbrunn palace in Vienna and was buried at the Habsburg tomb, the "Kapuziner Gruft." The restoration of the body of the Herzog von Reichsstadt from its burial place in Austria to the crypt of his father in Paris is one of the little-known and often overlooked actions undertaken by Adolf Hitler; it was designed as a gesture of reconciliation to show his respect for this icon of French history

'With the brief tour of Paris complete, Hitler's aesthetes were verbally charged by him with the job of making the new Berlin grander and more breath-taking than the beautiful French capital. *Reichsleiter* Martin Bormann was as usual to be responsible for executing all of Hitler's orders in the civilian sphere.

'Adolf Hitler then turned toward us – Speer, Breker and me: "For you a hard time begins: work and pressure, the developing of cities and monuments which are put into your trust. As far as I am able, and can spare the time, I will assist in your work. Bormann will assist me. Look after my artists and keep away from them anything that might hinder their work." And then again to us: "Put everything on Bormann's broad shoulders. He will stand by you."

'Adolf Hitler was quiet for a time before he said with a low voice: "At the Dome des Invalides, I was really aware only of Napoleon's sarcophagus at the open Ronda of the crypt. I fell strangely under the spell – for me everything else was meaningless."

'After a while, he explained to me why he wanted his grave site located in Munich, and why I should build it and in what form he wanted it to be built. It surprised me, but nonetheless, as a National Socialist, that reasoning made a lot of sense. It seemed no coincidence that we discussed that on the day of the victorious finale of the French battle it was certainly stimulated by the viewing of Napoleon's grave site. But in retrospect I suspect he was thinking about that for a long time.

'Hitler not surprisingly turned his attention once more to the present situation. He expressed his strong desire for a peace settlement – remembering the end of the destructive Thirty Years War and the Treaty of Westphalia which was signed in Munster. Was he comparing the recent troubles over nearly thirty turbulent years since 1914, and hoping to end it in the same way? Very possibly this was going through his mind.

'Silently we walked up and down the narrow path through the forest. Then Adolf Hitler stopped and said with great stress: "I want peace – and I will do anything to make peace! It is not yet too late. I will go to the limit of what is possible as long as the sacrifice and dignity of the German nation allows it. I know of superior things than waging war. If I just think about the loss of German blood – the finest always fall, the bravest and the ones willing to be sacrificed; their mission is to epitomise the nation.

'"I do not need to make a reputation by war-mongering like Churchill. I would like to make my name as a steward of the German people. I want to secure its unity and *Lebensraum*, to achieve National Socialism and shape the environment – add to it the new rebuilding of the German cities according to modern principles. I would like the people to be happy there and be proud of their town, their *Lebensraum*, and nation."

'After a while he said the peace should be signed in Munster. "I have my reasons for that – it would mean an historical caesura. When I now return to Munich, I have to take the necessary steps for the beginning of the rebuilding of the city – a forward-looking scheme in all areas of a city-wide development." I, and also Speer, would receive orders from him to start immediately with reconstruction. That naturally includes especially the central railway station and the Autobahn circle – they are the prerequisite of further rebuilding of the city. Dr. Todt will receive the order to make the necessary steel available. Then he repeated again: "I hope for Peace," and changed the subject.

'We all joined for the late dinner at the barracks. June 23 ended and the armistice began. The trumpet signals *Das Ganze halt* (All hold) arrived out of the night from varying distances. The windows were open. Setting himself apart from us, Adolf Hitler stood alone folding his hands. He gazed into the darkness. When, long after the signal, he returned to us, he had tears in his eyes. Quietly, with his typical languid movement, he said goodbye to us. He lifted his bent arm, the hand upwards-opened, like a greeting of friendship.

'Speer, Breker and Giesler then changed out of their military uniforms and left his entourage. Intriguingly Hitler's triumphal visit to Paris had lasted only three hours. However even in the moment of his greatest triumph, it seems that there was a lurking pre-occupation in the mind of Adolf Hitler. Paris was the glittering prize for Hitler and its capture, which had eluded the German generals during the First World War, was a stunning strategic achievement. Hitler confided to Giesler that the capture of the city made him happier than words could express, but Hitler's visit to Paris was remarkably brief. The tour began at 6 a.m., by 9 a.m. the tour was over, he would never return to France.'

Napoleon's tomb at Les Invalides.

Hitler leaves La Madeleine. On the left of the *Führer* are Speer and Giesler, on the right is Breker.

Chapter Eight

Hitler's Return to Flanders 26 June 1940

No sooner had the artists gone from Hitler's entourage than they were replaced by two former colleagues from Hitler's old regiment who were to accompany him on the next, and to Hitler, far more important, stage of his journey. Hitler had only hours to spare for his perfunctory Paris visit but, in June 1940, he would find a total of four days to re-visit the Great War battlefields. It was for this purpose he had summoned two former colleagues to accompany him on a second visit to an insignificant area of Flanders on the border of France and Belgium. Those trusted and hand-picked men were Max Amann and Ernst Schmidt. They embodied the idea of the *frontgemeinschaft* and also of *Kameradschaft*, the comradeship which Hitler so desperately sought to be associated with. As part of his entourage Hitler was also careful to include Heinrich Hoffmann, the man who had captured his first image of Hitler as an insignificant part the Munich crowd in August 1914 and who was now elevated to the role of Hitler's personal photographer. He was there to produce a photographic record of Hitler's triumphant return to the Great War battlefields.

What is highly significant is the fact that this visit was actually the second time during the momentous month of June 1940 that Hitler had found time to come to this militarily unimportant corner where France and Belgium meet. The real reason behind Hitler's second visit has been hotly debated ever since.

Hitler's Return to Flanders
26 June 1940

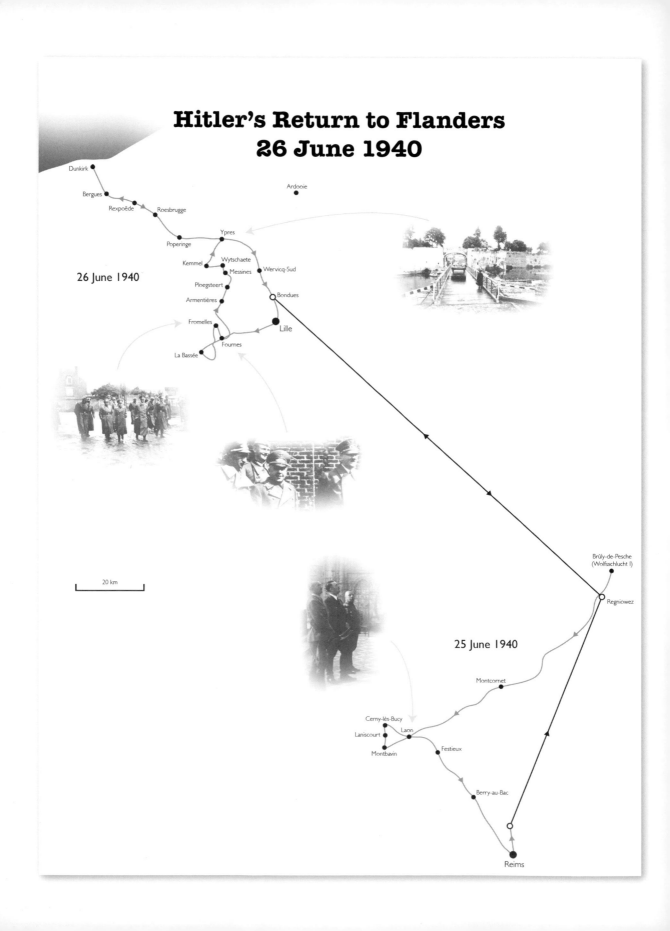

Dunkirk

Bergues

Rexpoëde

Roesbrugge

Ardooie

Ypres

Poperinge

26 June 1940

Kemmel

Wytschaete

Messines

Wervicq-Sud

Ploegsteert

Bondues

Armentières

Lille

Fromelles

Fournes

La Bassée

20 km

Brûly-de-Pesche
(Wolfsschlucht I)

Regniowez

25 June 1940

Montcornet

Cerny-lès-Bucy

Laniscourt

Laon

Montbavin

Festieux

Berry-au-Bac

Reims

Hitler, accompanied by Max Amann and Ernst Schmidt and aides, pictured shortly after the victory over France on 26 June 1940. The group were photographed on their tour to visit the positions they had occupied during Great War in Flanders.

In the church of Laon.

The procession soon took the air of a jovial motoring day trip, something which Hitler had enjoyed since he had first owned a car in the 1920s.

Hitler and his former colleagues visit a farm in Cerny-lès-Bucy, a village to the west of Laon where they had been billeted in late 1917 / early 1918.

Hitler and Amann during a visit to the fortress of Laniscourt. Amann had survived the Great War unscathed only to lose an arm in a hunting accident when, in 1931, he was shot by Hermann Göring

Hitler with (right to left) Max Amann, *Wehrmacht* adjutant Gerhard Engel, Ernst Schmidt and adjutant Julius Schaub on 26 April 1940 pictured at the location in Fournes, where Hitler, Schmidt and Amann had served together some 24 years earlier.

The party is captured in light hearted mood in the garden of the former billet in Fournes.

The three old comrades enter the village of Fromelles. This was the area in which Hitler spent the most time during the Great War.

Heinz Linge offers to clean Hitler's shoes with a cloth. Ernst Schmidt looks on.

Hitler and Amann inspecting the German bunkers near Fromelles. These bunkers and many similar structures have defied the efforts of local farmers to remove them and still dot the landscape today.

The three veterans contemplate the site of the former battlefield.

Hitler, in pensive mood, is snapped by Hoffmann during the afternoon of 26 June.

The ruins of the church at Messines, painted by Adolf Hitler in December 1914.

Hitler and his entourage entering Ypres via the temporary wooden bridge built by the German combat engineers at the Lille Gate.

The convoy makes it way through Ypres, passing down Gustave de Stuersstraat.

At around 4:30 p.m. on 26 June Hitler again enters the main square at Ypres.

The convoy driving through Dunkirk, the city still bears the scars of the recent combat.

The procession drives across the Grote Markt from Poperinge to the town hall.

On the return journey there was a sudden rainstorm. The convoy halted in Capelle-la-Grande, just south of Dunkirk, to deploy the folding roofs.

Hitler inspecting a German bunker unsuccessfully bombarded by the French.

On the Rhine bridge at Kehl. On the right of the *Führer* is the Supreme Commander of an Army, Senior General Dollmann.

Despite the heaviest artillery fire, this German bunker was undamaged.

Alongside Keitel and Bormann, Hitler inspects a French bunker after the bombardment.

In the Vosges at the gorge pass. The Supreme Commander of an Army, Senior General Dollman, explains the course of the heavy fighting to the *Führer*.

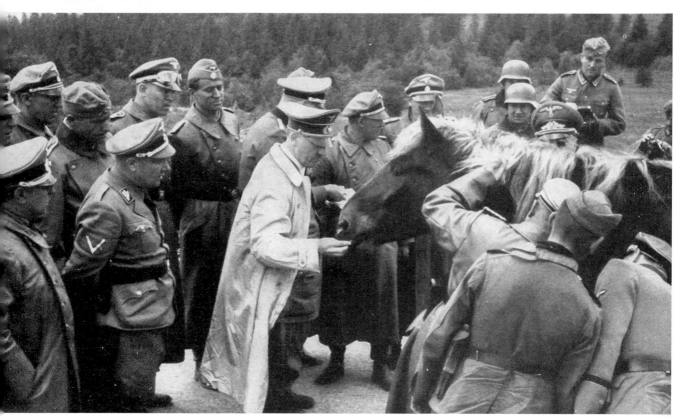

In the Vosges. A captured French war horse encounters the *Führer*.

Back on German soil Hitler is confronted with the mass hysteria which had been a feature of his political life since the twenties.

In June 1940 the crowds had a great deal to celebrate in the wake of what was then reckoned to be the greatest military victory in world history.

The cult of *Führer* worship extended to the German troops in the field. Hitler seen here in conversation with his victorious troops following the victory over the allies.

In the Strassburg cathedral.

Chapter Nine

In Conclusion

In the heady days of late June of 1940 the jubilant crowds that flocked the streets of Berlin and Munich to celebrate the fall of France hailed Adolf Hitler as a great German hero. They ecstatically proclaimed him the architect of the most stunning victory the world had ever seen and the febrile atmosphere was elevated further by *Generaloberst* Wilhelm Keitel who dubbed Hitler as 'the greatest general of all time'.

The National Socialist propaganda machine soon added another layer to the triumphalist celebrations: under the masterful control of Doctor Goebbels, the Nazis relentlessly trumpeted the idea that Hitler was a fearless fighter who, for four long years from 1914 to 1918, had served in the face of omnipresent danger. One of Goebbels' key target groups were the millions of new adherents to the Nazi party especially the legions of men who had served in the trenches, they formed the informal *frontgemeinschaft*, or brotherhood of frontline fighters. During the years of turmoil which had followed the Great War many of these men continued under arms and fought on as members of the *Freikorps*. Their support was vital to a party with paramilitary roots and they responded to the idea that Hitler was one of their number who enjoyed their *kameradschaft* – or fellowship.

Writing in the pages of his semi-autobiographical book *Mein Kampf* Hitler contributed his own highly selective account of his war-time service and the legend of the *Führer* as bold frontline fighter continued to grow. The Nazi propaganda master plan worked as intended and as a result of Goebbels' efforts millions of Germans, including the former soldiers who formed the *Nationalsocializter Deutscher Frontkämpferbund* (National Socialist League of German Frontline Fighters) unhesitatingly accepted the party line that Hitler had been a valiant hero fighting in the line of fire at the very frontline of the trenches.

By late June 1940 Hitler's position seemed unassailable, but even in his greatest hour of triumph, the debatable legacy of the Great War loomed over him. He was painfully aware that there were many who doubted his claims and accordingly he lived under the continual shadow of his opponents' allegations that his war record was wildly exaggerated and he was in fact nothing more than an *etapenschweine* (a rear area hog), and worse still, he was reputed to be a cowardly draft-dodger from the Austro-Hungarian army who had spent the First World War safely out of harm's way far behind the lines. For the man who was the figurehead of the *Nationalsocializter Deutscher Frontkämpferbund* this was an embarrassing weakness and it was to become a matter of huge personal importance to Adolf Hitler.

Throughout the twenties and into the thirties the Nazi propaganda machine had harnessed the support of former frontline soldiers by making an appeal to the spirit of *frontgemeinschaft*, the community of former frontline soldiers. It was vital therefore that in order to connect with this powerful and numerous group that Hitler was depicted as a bold hero of the battlefront. His own highly selective account in *Mein Kampf* shamelessly reinforced the legend of Hitler as a fearless warrior who was never far from the frontline trenches and worthy of *kameradschaft* or fellowship with the band of brothers who formed the *frontgemeinschaft*. Hitler has been fiercely criticised and has even been accused of hiding the fact that he was a *meldegänger*. This is certainly not the case: Hitler clearly refers to the fact that he was gassed in 1918 for the last time. It is fair to say however that this is the only reference to his actual role in the war.

Despite all of Goebbels' efforts, throughout the twenties and thirties there were constant whispers that the myth of Hitler the bold frontline fighter was a lie; a false concoction created by the Nazi spin doctors. Regardless of all of the Nazi boasts however, Hitler lived under the continual shadow of his opponents' allegations that he was not actually worthy of acceptance into the ranks of the *frontgemeinschaft* and had no real claim to be a part of the fellowship of his former colleagues. Furthermore he was targeted with the plausible claim that he was in fact nothing more than a cowardly draft-dodger from the Austro-Hungarian army who had spent the first world war out of harm's way far behind the lines.

His enemies pointed to the fact that Hitler was not a trench fighter, but actually held a cushy post as a regimental *meldegänger* (or messenger) who saved his own skin by ensuring that he was never promoted beyond the rank of Private. He was an *Etapenschweine* (a rear area hog) through and through.

Hitler easily won his court case; but even after Hitler assumed power the underground gossip continued.

Despite his court victory there were still gaps in Hitler's armour and his political opponents were able to continue their whispering campaign against him. However, in 1933 Hitler seized power and the Nazi machine was soon in full swing. Former colleagues such as Hans Mend and Korbinian Rutz, who did not toe the party line, soon found themselves in a concentration camp. Others like Alexander Moritz Frey, when the attentions of the SA grew too intimidating, were forced to flee into exile.

It was this continuing controversy which lurked on in the background during Hitler's first visit to Flanders in June 1940. That initial visit to the battlefields, which took place on 1 and 2 June 1940, may well have been a spontaneous personal pilgrimage, but it also seems to have provoked a new idea in Hitler's mind. France capitulated on 22 June 1940 and when he returned to France in triumph in late June 1940, Hitler seems to have been determined to finally lay an old ghost to rest. For Hitler, even 26 years, later the questions over his service in the Great War represented unfinished business; it seems he had a very public point to prove. It was for this reason that Hitler therefore resolved to spend so little time in Paris and so much time in Flanders. He had resolved that he would return to the battlefields of northern France and Flanders and would shamelessly use that second visit to cement his reputation as a member of, the *frontgemeinschaft* community of former front line fighters. In the light of this craving for acceptance we can now understand why Hitler brought with him two former colleagues from the 16th Reserve Infantry Regiment who had fought alongside him in the Great War.

On his second visit to Flanders that month Hitler, Amann and Schmidt visited Rijsel, Fournes, Fromelles, then drove through Armentiers to Ploegstreert then once more to Mesen and on Wytschaete and Kammel. The party then stopped in Ypres before driving to Dunkirk via Poperinge.

The stop over in Fournes allowed Hitler and his comrades to pose once more in the garden of the house in Fournes where the regimental messengers had once been based. The entourage then moved on to inspect the surviving bunkers at Fromelles before driving on through Ypres and on to Dunkirk returning through Poperinge, which had remained in British hands during the Great War. The *Führer* was serenaded by the music of a German military band.

As planned, the carefully photographed and choreographed visit had found its way into the pages of the propaganda press including cinema newsreels such as *Deutsche Wochenschau* and the cover of *Illustrierter Beobachter*, but the rumours concerning Hitler's war service were never dispelled, and today, over one hundred years later, we at last know the truth concerning Private Hitler's war. The second visit was a glorified photo opportunity: Hoffmann's photographs would provide proof of Hitler's return to the scenes of heroic deeds. The visit would then provide propaganda material which would reinforce the party line which depicted Hitler as the bold front line trench warrior and rightful leader of the *Nationalsocializter Deutscher Frontkämpferbund* which would also bring him closer to finally achieving acceptance into the ranks of the *frontgemeinschaft*.

Ultimately Hitler was to be disappointed, acceptance into the *kameradschaft* would never be his to enjoy. In just five years from his triumphal visit to France he would die a coward's death by his own hand, leaving the frontline fighters of the *Wehrmacht* in 1945 to soldier on in the war he had brought about. The men of 1945 had no option but to face the long march into captivity in Russia where many were forced into slave labour for ten years or more. That was the true nature of comradeship as practised by Adolf Hitler. Ironically Field Marshall Keitel exhibited the genuine spirit of *kameradschaft*. His sense of honour and duty led him to face the music and that road would lead to Nuremberg where, in 1946, he would face the hangman's noose.

The first troops returning home at the Brandenburg Gate after the victory over France.

Greater Germany welcomes its victorious troops home. A Brandenburg division returns to the Homeland after the victorious campaign in France.

Hitler passes through the lavishly decorated streets of the capital city to the Reich Chancellery.

The *Führer* and *Reichsmarschall* Göring on the historic balcony of the Reich Chancellery.

Jubilation surrounds the *Führer* in front of the Reich Chancellery on 6 July, 1940.

The historic Reichstag session on 19 July, 1940.

The *Führer's* thanks to his *Reichsmarschall*.

Preis: 20 Pfennig
*uland mit ermäß. Porto 30 Pfg.
Italien 2 Lire

DONNERSTAG, 13. JUNI 1940
15. JAHRGANG ∴ FOLGE 24

JB

VERLAG FRANZ EHER
NACHF. G.M.B.H.
MÜNCHEN 22

Neüe Aüfnahmen aüs Flandern

Aufnahme: PK. Hr. Hoffmann.   Der Führer in Ypern.
Der Oberste Befehlshaber nimmt eine Meldung seines Marine-Adjutanten, Fregattenkapitän von Puttkamer, entgegen.
Rechts: Hauptmann Engel, einer der Adjutanten der Wehrmacht beim Führer.

The real prize for Hitler was the feeling of proper belonging with his men. His carefully calculated propaganda exercise produced exactly what was required; headlines which glorified Hitler, validated his service in the Great War and tied the *Führer* to the fighting men of 1940.

Kriegsgräberfürsorge

Mitteilungen und Berichte vom Volksbund Deutsche Kriegsgräberfürsorge E.V.

Heft 8   Berlin, August 1940   20. Jahrgang

Presse Hoffmann, Berlin

Der Führer vor dem Deutschen Ehrenmal Langemarck

Jubel um den Führer bei der Ankunft vor dem Ehrenfriedhof der deutschen Jugend in Langemarck.

Der Führer
bei der
Truppe in Flandern

Der Führer am 2. Juni auf der Vimyhöhe
Im Hintergrund das kanadische Weltkriegstotenmal, das nach einer Meldung des englischen Lügenministers Duff Cooper von den „deutschen Barbaren" angeblich zerstört wurde. Ein schlagendes Bilddokument für die schamlose Verlogenheit der englischen Propaganda. Unser Bild zeigt den Führer, der den Generalmajor Rommel auf der Vimyhöhe begrüßt.

Der Führer im Gespräch mit General der Infanterie Strauß.
Rechts der Chef des Oberkommandos der Wehrmacht, Generaloberst